Poems
for Teaching
in the
Content Areas

75 Powerful Poems to Enhance
Your History, Geography, Science,
and Math Lessons

J. Patrick Lewis
Teaching Ideas by Laura Robb

New York • Toronto • London • Auckland • Sydney
Mexico City • New Delhi • Hong Kong • Buenos Aires

Teaching
Resources

Dedication

This book is for those teachers not quite smitten with poetry and for others who are enchanted by poetry but, like me, missed out on it in school. —J.P.L.

With love for Lloyd —L.R.

Scholastic grants teachers permission to photocopy the reproducible pages from this book for classroom use. No other part of this publication may be reproduced in whole or in part, or stored in a retrieval system, or transmitted in any form or by any means, electronic, mechanical, photocopying, recording, or otherwise, without permission of the publisher. For information regarding permission, write to Scholastic Inc., 557 Broadway, New York, NY 10012.

Cover design by Maria Lilja
Interior design by Sarah Morrow

Copyright © 2007 by J. Patrick Lewis
All rights reserved. Published by Scholastic Inc.
Printed in the U.S.A.
ISBN-13 978-0-439-89603-0
ISBN 0-439-89603-7

1 2 3 4 5 6 7 8 9 10   40   13 12 11 10 09 08 07

Table of Contents

SECTION 3: *Science* 60

SECTION 4: *Math* 82

Introduction

by Laura Robb

I became acquainted with J. Patrick Lewis more than a dozen years ago through his poetry, which I instantly adored. Over the years, I became a collector of his poetry books, and I have had the opportunity to collaborate with him on programs for the National Council of Teachers of English (NCTE) and the International Reading Association (IRA). In 2005, I bumped into Pat at NCTE in Pittsburgh, Pennsylvania. We were both sipping wine at a Scholastic party and spent time trading family stories. Then, the conversation turned to poetry for content subjects. I explained to Pat that I was using poetry in content classes to connect students to topics in history, geography, science, and math. My problem was that I needed poems that related to specific topics, such as variables in math, the Civil War, biology, and so on. While people around us chatted and ate cheese and crackers, Pat and I sat at a table and jotted down ideas for this book on several napkins. Then, we presented our plan to Terry Cooper, the editor-in-chief of Scholastic Teaching Resources, and she loved it. And so, that evening, this book was born.

Now, two years later, I'm sitting at my computer, writing the introduction to this collection of poetry by Pat and thinking back on that evening and on the many content classes I've observed over the years. These observations have demonstrated to me the need for poems about history, geography, science, and math, poems that breathe life into the facts students learn and make them relevant by connecting them to issues in our world.

Recently, I spent three days observing a seventh-grade history class as they learned about the Civil War. These three days transported me back to my own middle and high school content area classes. Like most of the students I observed, I absorbed facts about the topic only if it interested me; otherwise I tuned out. In this history class, I could easily see that most of the boys were more engaged with the Civil War battles than the girls. Some students took no notes and stared out the window or doodled on the paper meant for note-taking.

I recognized these behaviors from my middle school days. Spending class after class memorizing names, dates, and long lists of vocabulary words in history, geography, or science was tedious and did not help me understand or connect to the topic being studied. Movies often helped my friends and me remember all the facts we'd been studying. For instance, I vividly recall watching *All Quiet on the Western Front* when studying World War I. Having a visual along with a storyline provided me with a context in which to fit together and think about the facts. Of course, showing a movie on every topic you teach is not feasible, but fortunately there are other ways to provide students with a memorable context for your content. Reading aloud part of a diary entry, letters written by soldiers to family and friends, a short story, a historical novel, an essay, a newspaper article, or a poem can help students imagine and visualize the information to be learned.

Like you, I want students to learn and remember your subject's content. Like you, I want students to think with and analyze learned information so that the facts become meaningful and transferable to other situations. That's why I believe my goals as a reading teacher and your goals as a content area teacher are the same. I offer these poems as a way to help us meet our goals of creating strong readers and thinkers.

The Benefits of Using Poetry to Teach Content

At this point, you're probably wondering, Why a collection of poems for history, geography, science, and math? First, the poems bring a human element and a personal, often humorous touch to the topics you are studying, which helps students retain information and vocabulary—they now have vivid and/or humorous mental images that forge remembering connections. For example, in "George Washington Carver" (page 22), the conversation between Carver and God has salty humor that leads us to see Carver's inventive and creative mind, which we might not fully appreciate by simply memorizing his name and the dates of his creations.

Second, poems are short and cut to the heart of a topic. In just a few minutes you can use a poem to connect students to your content topic in powerful and memorable ways. "Chromosome Poem," for instance, is a catchy way to remember some of the traits chromosomes are responsible for determining. Then as students learn more about the topics, they link new information to their own lives and make connections to other texts and experiences.

Third, and perhaps most important, poetry helps students explore important issues in your content area, issues that extend beyond the classroom into their lives, communities, and the world. This volume contains poems on war, immigration, natural disasters, and technology that are sure to spark lively discussions that can enhance the content you're teaching. It's this stepping beyond the facts—making connections, analyzing information, and creating new understandings—that enables students to "get into" your subject and see its relevance to their lives and their world.

Using the poems to raise issues is a key teaching idea that asks students to think with the facts about a topic. I recommend raising issues wherever possible because issues invite students to use the facts gathered to create new understandings and develop social and community responsibility.

Raising Issues Through Poetry

Let me illustrate this idea by asking you to step inside a seventh-grade American history class as Mr. Bell, the teacher, uses one of Pat's poems in this collection (page 15) to raise the issue of loss in war and to personalize the death and carnage that seems so remote when reading the bare facts in a textbook. To begin, Mr. Bell read the poem from an overhead transparency two times.

The Skull

by J. Patrick Lewis

Nine hundred died at Hatchie's Bridge—a mere
Stone in the bloody mountain of brothers dead—
And five years on, a boy, Shane Armistead,
Walking the ghostly meadow thick with deer,
Stumbled, hurtling him into big bluestem.
A hawk circled a thermal beside the sun
As Shane, moaning and cursing to no one,
Brushed a mask of skull. It was one of them—
Blue or gray. But who could say? Wide eye
Sockets like caves, mud-mottled teeth, a bee-
Line fracture half the height of Tennessee
Parted the bone. The boy began to cry.
This sky the only witness to take the stand:
The son was holding his father in his hand.

First, Mr. Bell gives students one minute to write three or four words and phrases that pop into their minds after hearing the poem. He then invites them to share their words with the class; many are quite powerful: *horrifying, painful, destructive, no glory in war, extreme loss, realistic, lonely.* Next, students talk in pairs to connect the poem to the issue of loss during war. I've included some of their comments so you can see the insights this short but gripping poem created.

"It made me see that it's not just names and news reports like in Iraq, but it's people losing family and friends."

"It made me feel for the boy and his dad. Otherwise, war dead are so not personal that you can't relate to what's happening."

"I think the poem made me see that with all the violence on TV and the movies and the reporting of war deaths every day, I have lost my feelings about senseless death."

The entire lesson took five minutes. It set a tone for the study of the battles of the Civil War and at the same time raised the issue of loss during war, which led students to think of ways to make peace instead of war and to consider whether war is inevitable. These issues and discussions are relevant to our volatile times and make learning about the Civil War feel important and meaningful for all students. Taking three to five minutes to connect your students to your content can make all the difference in their desire to learn. I've included, in the next section, some common teaching methods that will work for you no matter which poem you use. As you read on, consider these suggestions and adapt them to your teaching style and needs.

A Quick and Easy Routine for Using the Poems in Your Class

In four or five minutes, you can read aloud a poem and have a brief discussion with students that can raise key issues to guide their study of a topic. Here is a simple routine to help you get started.

1. Make an overhead transparency of the poem and enough copies so pairs can share.
2. Distribute the copies to partners and place the poem on an overhead projector. Read it aloud twice.
3. Invite students to jot down their immediate response by noting words and phrases that popped into their minds as you read aloud.
4. Have students exchange their thoughts with their partners. Then ask pairs to share their findings with the entire class.
5. Ask students to write in their notebooks the connections they made to your subject, the issues the poem raised, or any insights into a specific topic that the poem helped them understand.

Once you're ready to move beyond this brief but effective framework, you can offer students ideas for projects and writing that you'll find in each section's introduction.

Navigating the Introductions to Each Content Area

For each of the four content sections in this collection of original poems, I provide a brief introduction, followed by a section that contains four projects based on the poems—projects that ask students to complete additional research and explore concepts and ideas. I've addressed these directly to students so you can photocopy the ideas and let students choose projects that interest them. In addition, you'll find three writing ideas for students. If you want to go beyond the five-minute lesson framework described above, start with the projects and writing ideas I've suggested, then invite your students to suggest their own research and writing projects based on any of the poems they've read and discussed or on topics being studied. When students share this kind of responsibility with you, they develop a commitment to learning the information and using it to complete a project that makes the information relevant to them. Students can work on these projects during class time, after completing required work, in a study hall or library period, or for homework.

You can also enlist the English teacher on your team to use the poems as a springboard for students to compose their own poetry, which will further enrich their understanding of your content. I think you'll find that reading content poetry combined with learning content information can provide the connections that inspire your students to learn, think with the facts, and create new understandings.

Poems for Teaching in the Content Areas by J. Patrick Lewis   Scholastic Teaching Resources

Using Issues and Themes to Build Comprehension

In addition to relating to the topics you teach, many of the poems in this collection address issues and themes that are part of our lives today. Asking students to connect a theme or issue to a poem and then explain how they arrived at the connection encourages them to use facts and details while thinking at high levels.

One way to begin incorporating issues and themes is to distribute a list of them to students; see my sample list in the box on the right. Organize students into pairs, and invite them to link one or more poems to an issue or theme. Explain that partners will have to present their connections to the class and support these with details from the poems. Note that some poems will relate to two issues or themes. For example, "Tsunami" (page 40) relates to the theme of change and the issue of natural disasters. You can easily extend this activity to include other texts students are using.

Themes/Issues

War

Death

Racism

Discrimination

Human Rights

Justice/Injustice

The Holocaust

Change

Immigration

Family

Disasters

Ecology

Preserving the Earth's Air

Genetic Engineering

Natural Wonders

Exploration

Weather Changes

Evolution

Biology

Space Exploration

History

Suggestions for Teaching With the History Poems

"What I want is, Facts. Teach these boys and girls nothing but Facts. Facts alone are wanted in life. Plant nothing else, and root out everything else," declared Thomas Gradgrind in Charles Dickens's novel, *Hard Times*. If Mr. Gradgrind could come to life and chat with me, he and I would have a major disagreement about whether or not learning facts is the ultimate goal of studying history. "Just the facts" and nothing more is boring. But, when we teachers invite students to think about a poem and explore the significance of historical events to the people who lived through them, we help students consider the facts in different contexts. Then we can ask students to connect their understandings to their own lives and contemporary world issues, making the information relevant and useful.

And isn't that what the study of history is all about?

The poems in this collection help your students move beyond the facts by giving voice to fictional characters who lived through a historical event, such as Hans Knorr and Elijah Weiss in the "Battle of Argonne Forest, 1918" (page 31). Pat personalizes historical events with details that make them come alive. For instance, in "With All Deliberate Speed" (page 25) he includes the name of Linda Brown's school and a description of its condition: "textbooks out of date and dumb." Such details link readers to Linda Brown and her experience while enabling them to make connections to the wide variation of building conditions and learning materials found in today's schools. With these connections, students can raise their level of social responsibility and perhaps even work for positive change in their communities.

An Important Note About the History Poems

You will find poems such as "You Were Selected for the Gas Chambers If . . ." (page 32) and "The Moth" (page 12) stir powerful feelings and ignite students' thinking engines, which is good. Since these poems are more appropriate for older students, I've placed an asterisk (*) next to the title and suggested suitable grade levels at the bottom of the page.

Student Projects and Writing Ideas

Here are some ways to use the poems in this section to start meaningful discussions and to inspire questions to research on the Internet. Share your discoveries with classmates.

Create a Web Site

Choose a group of poems that deal with the same topic, such as the Civil War or immigration. Post the poems on the Web site along with comments about them that you've collected from classmates. Find and post images and articles from newspapers that reported the event when it happened. If there were no newspapers during that period, write an original news article as if you were there.

Podcast Interviews

Choose a poem that raised questions for you about certain issues and problems. Discuss these with a partner and then write down three or four questions that grew out of your discussion. Next, record the poem. Then read the questions you and your partner created and discuss each one.

Step Into the Poem

Use the Internet to research a time period reflected in a poem or group of poems. Search for diaries, interviews, journal entries, and other first-hand accounts that give you insight into how people felt when the event in the poem occurred. Then connect the event to a similar problem or issue we face today.

Prepare an oral presentation to show how people reacted to and felt about the event in the poem. You can also prepare a cartoon, poster, or illustrated timeline of the event to use with your presentation. For instance, you might use "The Irish Immigrant" and "The Jewish Immigrant" to think about the issues raised by immigration today.

Link a Poem or Group of Poems to Today's World

Select three or four poems about war to discuss with a partner or a small group. Discuss how the details in the poems relate to wars that are part of today's world. Then explore the issues that these details raise. For example, in "The Skull" you discover how the Civil War caused a child to lose his father and the pain the son feels when he discovers his dad's skull. In Iraq and Afghanistan, parents have lost children and children have lost parents. Death and lost life are the inglorious aspects of war. Could these losses help you find other ways to solve conflicts that seem irreconcilable?

Writing Ideas

Here are three ideas to start you composing your own poems or other kinds of writing. You might wish to read your poems to the class. You can publish them on a bulletin board in your class or hall or post them on your school's Web site.

1. **Write a letter** to a historical figure you've been studying or to a person mentioned in one of the history poems that we've read. In your letter, discuss what you've learned and outline your position on issues the person or poem raises, such as the destruction of war, genocide, equal rights, and so on.

2. **Write a list poem** about a holiday that's historical, such as July 4, Flag Day, Presidents' Day, Veterans Day, and so on. Create a list of your associations with and feelings about the holiday. Then select and organize those you want to include in your poem.

3. **Use a photograph** of a historical event as inspiration for a poem or short article, pointing out the issues and problems the photograph raises as well as your position on those issues. You can find photos in your textbook, on the Internet, in newspapers, magazines, and informational texts.

The Moth *

The Battle of Bull Run
July 21, 1861

From the rough shade
of Private Lemuel Benniger's
horsehair blanket, she watched
the shoutingchokingdying men
falling like barrels of broken
sticks down Henry House Hill.

She dragged her chalk wings
across the mud-crusted boot
of a 14-year-old whipsaw boy
overrun by the 33rd Virginia Infantry.

When screaming painted
the blood-cloud sky, she flew
erratically to the left ear of Corporal
Endicott Frye, fifteen feet
from Corporal Frye.

From there it was a short flight
to a chinaberry tree where she
waged war with a Slave Dart moth,

Then surveyed the field of 5,000
dead or wished-to-be,
and heard one gray captain mutter,
his leg all but torn away,
"I knew we could count on General
Beauregard to pull us through."

---

* Recommended for grades 7 and up.

Poems for Teaching in the Content Areas by J. Patrick Lewis   Scholastic Teaching Resources

Diary of Whit Berry, Corporal, Sharpshooter, Army of the United States *

Battle of Monocacy
Frederick, Maryland
July 9, 1864

I drew a killshot bead on Jubal Early,
Confederate general barking at the rear,
But something spooked me. I had not securely
Settled on courage or outmaneuvered fear.
Blue ragtags fell like hail. We thought salvation
Arrived by Burnside's bullet to the brain.
Our troops, lacking in all but determination,
Lay lifeless now, their morgue a mercy train.
To slow Early's advance, that was the mission:
He looked to capture Washington that day.
General Lew Wallace said on one condition:
What you would take, we will not give away.
Two thousand dead on both sides spelled defeat—
Rebs won the battle, but their spoils? Retreat.

* Recommended for grades 5 and up.

William Beau Dare *

Civil War Confederate Deserter, 2nd Tennessee Mounted Infantry, 1863

What will it be tonight, William Beau Dare?
You say, *C'est la vie* , and they say, *C'est la guerre.*

> *I'll fluff me a pillow here under the stars*
> *And capture the glitter in vinegar jars.*

Who will you take along, William Beau Dare,
Strangers, your neighbors or nearest of kin?

> *I'll take for companion a tipple of tea,*
> *Two dollars, an onion, a book on the sea.*

What are you looking for, William Beau Dare?
They'll hunt you from misery back to despair.

> *There's only one mystery that matters to me—*
> *Why life is the torment it turned out to be.*

What are you fearful of, William Beau Dare,
The bullet, the rope, or the winds of warfare?

> *Taking my orders from bungling Bragg,*
> *A General whose honor dishonors the flag.*

Where are you going to, William Beau Dare?
You'll find little comfort. There's little to spare.

> *Existence is nothing inside this cage.*
> *How much have we missed of our easy age?*

When will we hear from you, William Beau Dare,
The first of Begone or the last of Beware?

> *I'll write you a letter in blood and ink*
> *Of journeys to nowhere, then see what you think.*

What if it's nevermore, William Beau Dare?
What if you're living another nightmare?

> *Remember a boy to his dear old mum—*
> *I'll be waitin' for her in kingdom come.*

---

* Recommended for grades 7 and up.

Poems for Teaching in the Content Areas by J. Patrick Lewis   Scholastic Teaching Resources

The Skull *

1867

Nine hundred died at Hatchie's Bridge—a mere
Stone in the bloody mountain of brothers dead—
And five years on, a boy, Shane Armistead,
Walking the ghostly meadow thick with deer,
Stumbled, hurtling him into big bluestem.
A hawk circled a thermal beside the sun
As Shane, moaning and cursing to no one,
Brushed a mask of skull. It was one of them—
Blue or gray. But who could say? Wide eye
Sockets like caves, mud-mottled teeth, a bee-
Line fracture half the height of Tennessee
Parted the bone. The boy began to cry.
This sky the only witness to take the stand:
The son was holding his father in his hand.

---

* Recommended for grades 7 and up.

From the Ghost Dance to the Wicked Witch

1890–1900

Shuffling akimbo,
the Modoc eyed the northern lights.
Waiting for redemption, the Arapaho
stopped shooting their horses.
Each Cheyenne sang to his own blade
of grass. The Walapai imagined
wind was their destroyer.
Rain turns white hearts to water,
sang the Crow, prone to fancy.
By corn harvest time they will be gone,
said the Apache, alive to the Contraries.
Freezing in wickiups, the Lakota Sioux
stayed pure. And the rains came suddenly
from the barrels of the Hotchkiss guns.

Five days after Wounded Knee,
the Aberdeen (S.D.) Pioneer ran an editorial:
Having wronged them for centuries we had better,
in order to protect our civilization,
follow it up by one more wrong
and wipe these untamed and untamable (sic)
creatures from the face of the earth.
Its author, then an unknown genius of fantasy,
would delight the white world ten years later
with *The Wonderful Wizard of Oz*.

Poems for Teaching in the Content Areas by J. Patrick Lewis   Scholastic Teaching Resources

Visions of the West *

Out along the broken rim of history,
miles from camp and caution,
three young cowboys see across the gorge
the magnificent sockeye as it skies
on the electric moment, flying up
in spray, shelving on the glass niagara.
This is the final act above the falls.

The spent rose-fish roes the water
and clatters the stone, announcing birth
and grief until she is out of her element.

A blackheart marten snakes through
the wet winds along the riverbank, bobbing
and weaving. He rattles the salmon viciously,
spanking the air. She glistens with fever
in his ragged vice.

Suddenly, beyond the small spectacle,
the riders stare like mute witnesses
at the bonneted warrior galloping along
the border of time on a wisp of white pony.

Said one, *"I believe he is their ancestor*
returning from a thousand years' sleep
to avenge Wounded Knee."

And the stained earth tilted fearfully
into the new century.

---

* Recommended for grades 6 and up.

If Women Get the Vote

19th Amendment
Ratified August 18, 1920

There's no use to pretend,
The world's about to end,
If women get the vote.

The Catholics'll get in,
The blacks and Jews'll win,
If women get the vote.

Who wants to take the chance
That they'll be wearing pants,
If women get the vote?

Egads, I do believe
They might just up and leave,
If women get the vote.

And once their muscle's flexed,
What horror happens next,
If women get the vote?

Now just imagine, friend,
The message this will send.
There's no use to pretend,
We know the world will end,
If women get the vote.

Poet's note: This poem is obviously ironic.

Poems for Teaching in the Content Areas by J. Patrick Lewis   Scholastic Teaching Resources

The Irish Immigrant

It's not the siren song of common prayer
That summons up the confidence to go.
He hears the ancient voice of some forebear,

A victim of repression and despair,
Who tells him everything he needs to know.
It's not the siren song of common prayer.

From Dublin to the coast of County Clare,
The world that beckons through the radio
Is but the ancient voice of some forebear

Repeating "Opportunity is there!
Git on with it, me lad, you'll miss the show."
It's not the siren song of common prayer.

"Hearts are sad, potato cellars bare,
The future's quick as coffins down below."
He hears the ancient voice of his forebear.

"Us Irish niver knew a millionaire.
Git goin', even if you have to row"
Is not the siren song of common prayer.
He hears the ancient voice of his forebear.

The Jewish Immigrant

She walked so slowly off the ship the plank
barely moved.
The spectacle unhinged her! She went blank
And stared down at the dock as if to thank
Someone she loved.

What scent of this new land assaulted first?
The steel, the rust!
Old fishmongers, young stevedores, all cursed
In gibberish to which she was unversed.
Her wanderlust—

She'd waited years!—remained high-spirited.
As one displaced,
She thought she knew what danger lay ahead—
Deep hatred of the Jews, poverty and dread.
She'd learn to face

The world. Today she knows that she would choose
Again that time
When hundreds of thousands of Polish Jews,
Desperate families with nothing left to lose,
Survived the climb.

Poems for Teaching in the Content Areas by J. Patrick Lewis   Scholastic Teaching Resources

America Enters World War II *

When Franklin D. Roosevelt locked
the National Fear in a safe and took
the box of Fortitude from the cupboard
of Resolve, Europe held its breath.

There were those in their fiery hats
who insisted that he steer the ship
of state through the Straits of Denial.

A congress of clouds met just above.
The foe formed into a foe.
The President was undaunted,
The Commander-in-Chief of his soul.

---

* Recommended for grades 6 and up.

Poet's note: "A congress of clouds met just above./The foe formed into a foe." This is a poetic way of saying that
it took more than two years before America entered the war against Hitler. "A congress of clouds"
suggests that we wavered in our decision to go to war.

George Washington Carver

Soil Scientist
c. 1865–1943

Well, one day Mr. Carver asked
The Lord to tell him all
About the misty universe,
Secrets great and small.

"You want to know too much," God said,
And graciously declined.
But Mr. Carver wanted any
Answers he could find.

So Mr. Carver said, "I wonder
If You could afford
To tell me just one secret of
The humble peanut, Lord."

"The peanut!" God replied. "Why, that's
About the perfect size
For Mr. Carver, Soil
Scientist, to analyze."

He analyzed the peanut
And the sweet potato too,
Inventing many things like paints,
Linoleum, shampoo,

And peanut butter, vinegar,
Insecticide and yeast.
"Sometimes," he said, "you find the
Secrets best among the least."

Poems for Teaching in the Content Areas by J. Patrick Lewis   Scholastic Teaching Resources

The Elder

[Found Poem]
Black Elk
Sioux Holy Man
1863–1950

Once the two-leggeds
And the four-leggeds lived
Together like relatives.
And the bison were so many
That they could not be counted.
But sometimes the White Man
Did not even take the hides,
Only the tongues. Sometimes
They did not even take the tongues;
They just killed and killed
Because they liked to do that.
When the White Man came,
They made little islands for us.
It was like some fearful thing in a fog.

Battle of Chosin

November 26,–December 13, 1950
Korea

No soldier can forget a distant planet,
So cold a crater cold itself went numb.
The mind of a Marine, a will of granite
Could not unmask the misery to come.
The Chinese swept over us like a wave!
Surrounded and outnumbered five to one,
We spit fear in the eye. A frozen grave—
The end of our undoing—was undone.

Facing the senseless casualties of war,
Commander Chesty Puller, 1st Marines,
Retook the 7th Infantry's machines.
We broke out of the Chosin reservoir,
Bearing the brutal lesson of those hills:
What hope does not abandon, winter kills.

Poems for Teaching in the Content Areas by J. Patrick Lewis   Scholastic Teaching Resources

"With All Deliberate Speed"

Brown v. Board of Education
1954

That's third grader Linda Brown over there,
skipping along through the railroad switching yard.
And a mile beyond her house is Monroe Elementary
School where the kids take turns with textbooks
out of date and dumb.

Over here, just seven blocks away from Linda's house,
is Sumner Elementary School (no Lindas allowed)
where rumor has it that a kid can even pack a rainbow
in his lunchbox.

And just above all of Topeka floats a question it seems
can only be answered by certain men in black robes.
The white robes have already decided.

And then, when Linda finds a new home in middle school,
the black robes figure it's time to open a few elementary
windows, air the place out, so no more separate tomfoolery
can ever be equal.

Hallelujah, says Linda Brown and Linda Brown's folks
and Linda Brown's neighbors, *What took so long?*

But twenty-five years later, Linda Brown Smith realizes
new winds are still not welcome everywhere, so why not take
the windows out altogether. *Let it rain*, she says, *let it rain
and rain, not white rain, not black rain, just plain old rain.*

The Vietcong Tunnels *

Now some were wide and some were deep,
But all of them snick-snaked along
Into your very fitful sleep,
The tunnels of the Vietcong.

And they were dug to fight the war
Americans had thought was right.
The staunch belief they held before
They learned where they were sent to fight:

A jungle that defied all maps.
The wicked trees, the tangled vines
Disguised so many booby traps
And other anti-human mines.

And there were those G.I.'s who crawled
Inside the holes like stealthy cats,
Individuals who were called
Many things and tunnel rats.

What, you might ask, did G.I.'s do
Inside the burrow of the foe?
Well, this was war, that much is true,
But it was many years ago.

We quit the war and stopped the bomb,
Trying now to get along.
Still spidered under Vietnam?
The tunnels of the Vietcong.

* Recommended for grades 6 and up.

Poems for Teaching in the Content Areas by J. Patrick Lewis   Scholastic Teaching Resources

Chan Chim in Grosse Pointe *

Father arranged her stay with us
through Immigration. Yet in a blue
month, she's shown no gratitude
for a country club atmosphere.

Her face still wears the war in Cambodia.
Fire dreams of sons, an ancient daughter,
waken her, shaking, afraid to break
the imperial air.

A ravaged peasant, she looks Chinese
speaks a bit of English, an old woman
at thirty-seven. Ebony eyes, gossamer
hair, her mouth, her sorrow.

Evenings, when the china and the children
have been put to bed, she stares at the TV,
numbed to the guns, yet lit with a soft
expectancy, unaccustomed to continual
laughter.

She remembers that men liked to amuse
themselves by throwing hand grenades
under water buffaloes just to see how high
water buffaloes can fly.

* Recommended for grades 7 and up.

Veterans Day

November 11

World Wars erased so many lives
When angry bullets caught them.
We stand today to honor those
Who stood, unbowed, and fought them.

Let grief, hope and intensity
Combine to show another
Path, inimical to a war—
That there not be another.

Poems for Teaching in the Content Areas by J. Patrick Lewis   Scholastic Teaching Resources

Cyclops, One-Eyed Giant

A
1-eyed
giant called
the Cyclops once
ate a handful of tasty
Greeks. He would have
eaten them all like gyro sand-
wiches since he had them trapped
in his cave. But Ulysses, their leader,
had a brilliant idea for escape. My name is
Noman, he told the Cyclops. When Noman offered
the giant strong wine, it put him fast asleep. The men
then struck the sleeping giant in his bloodshot eye, blind-
ing him with a hot spear point shaped like this poem.
Roaring to his brother Cyclopes, the giant said, *Noman
is hurting me.* But if no man is hurting you, then all must
be well, they replied from beyond the cave, and then
they departed. The next morning, the blind giant rolled
the massive stone from the entrance to his cave to let
his sheep out to graze. That's when Ulysses' men took
hold of the woolly sheep bellies. The Cyclops felt only
the sheeps' backs as they passed by, trying to make
certain that Noman and his men were still his prisoners
inside the cave. But hidden under the fleece, the Greeks
boldly *and* sheepishly escaped to safety. The moral:
Brains usually win out over brawn, which is the very
sharp point of this story told ever so many centuries ago.

Letter to Galileo From His Daughter, Sister Maria Celeste

My Illustrious Lord Father,

Whose time of troubles never seems to cease,
You are and shall remain my universe,
Languishing though you must under a curse
Imposed by ignorance. Rest, Sire, release
Your soul to Him Who Is Our Centerpiece,
Even as you, against all odds, reverse
The myth-makers. For better or for worse,
I send you love in trifles, piece by piece—
Your laundered shirts, my marzipan (godsend!),
Translations of your notes, a book of days,
A soothing tonic that should help you mend
Your loneliness with solitude, a friend.
Remember this, your constant reader prays,
And so she shall unto our worldly end.

From San Matteo,
January, 1633

S. Maria Celeste

Poems for Teaching in the Content Areas by J. Patrick Lewis   Scholastic Teaching Resources

Battle of Argonne Forest, 1918 *

In war's last gasp, the Battle of Argonne,
a bootless young G.I., Elijah Weiss,
machine gunner out on patrol at dawn,
was standing up, asleep, and paid the price.
A German sniper bullet sent the brave
Marine rolling downhill for what seemed miles
through ferny forest to a watery grave,
his lifeless hands extended, like a child's.

Private Hans Knorr, nineteen and three days missing,
trembling in that mad bunker, Desperation,
heard before he felt the mortars hissing
that hurtled him to that same dread location.
In life, when reason rules, could they have been
acquaintances the world would keep from harm—
two boys war kept from ever being men,
in death, now deathless comrades arm in arm?

---

* Recommended for grades 5 and up.

You Were Selected
For the Gas Chambers If...*

You were a Jew

You had a limp

You had a scar

You wore a beard

You had a scratch on your leg

You were pregnant

You wore broken glasses

You wore glasses

You were a Jew

You were a twin

You were a child

You were a communist

You were a homosexual

You ran

You hid

You laughed

You cried

You were sick, weak and old

You were less than human

You were a Jew

* Recommended for grades 7 and up.

Poems for Teaching in the Content Areas by J. Patrick Lewis   Scholastic Teaching Resources

The Afternoon of the Hunchback and His Son *

Auschwitz/Birkenau, 1943

They had no time to pack their lives in teacups.
Off the cattle-train, Jews went right or left,
to death or to work. But two specimens were
spared till the end of an afternoon.

They were examined in the dissection room
by the soothing healer-killer Nyiszli. *Retarded,
rickets*, he said to the hunchback. *Hypomelia,
no foot muscles*, he said to the lame boy,
who could not speak for shaking. *You can walk
perfectly well with these orthopedic socks.*

Stewed beef with macaroni was brought in—
their last supper. The hunchback and his son ate
ravenously. In the cupboard, a decapitated head
nodded. Several eyeballs rolled around in a glass
dish as if they had seen this all before. A young girl's
skeleton worked her jaw into a horrifying scream
that no one heard. The revolver cracked twice,
sending them both to a black sea.

Josef Mengele, the Angel of Death, arrived after
having dispatched ten thousand Jews before breakfast.
He ordered the bodies boiled in water. But the two
sets of misshapen bones sent to Berlin on behalf
of science were not quite complete. A guard had
pocketed one crooked finger bone, which would
provide the missing piece in his son's collection.

* Recommended for grades 7 and up.

In Fields of Woe

Cesar Chavez
Migrant Worker Activist
1927–1993

There once was a simple wizard
Who walked a simple path
And tasted bitter harvest
And dined on grapes of wrath
He could not wrap the evening
In scarves on firefly nights
Or mystify six moonbeams
Or dizzy the world in lights
But faith he learned from labor
And grit he taught the boss
Made every single neighbor
Refuse the double-cross
You did not see him waver
A fever to the bone
Kept him from seeking favor
He worked out on his own
There once was a simple wizard
Who knew no sleight of hand
And I am the simple wizard
And here I make my stand

Poems for Teaching in the Content Areas by J. Patrick Lewis   Scholastic Teaching Resources

The Last Man Killed at the Berlin Wall *

Chris Gueffroy
February 6, 1989

It was a cold day to die,
a rotten day to die
along the Britz District canal.
Chris Gueffroy climbed a dream,
the last lattice fence to West Berlin
and freedom, certain that Befehl 101,
the shoot-to-kill order that stopped
260 escaping Germans, had been lifted.

Ten bullets slammed into Gueffroy's heart.

Four guards were given a holiday
and 150 marks each. Later, they were tried
for murder. Ingo Heinrich, Gueffroy's
executioner, was sentenced to three
and a half years in prison, but later released.

Nine months later, on November 9th,
Germans smashed the wall to pieces.
It was the fifty-first anniversary of *Kristallnacht*,
the night the Nazis vandalized so many Jewish
stores and synagogues, smashing them to pieces.

---

* Recommended for grades 7 and up.

Rules of History?

The fatter the king, the thinner the serf.
The longer the reign, the duller the pain.
The stronger the crown, the weaker the law.
The fainter the dream, the slimmer the hope.

The darker the night, the deeper the fear.
The blacker the skin, the whiter the hate.
The colder the sin, the hotter the fire.
The taller the tree, the thicker the rope.

The bigger the bomb, the quicker the dead.
The larger the war, the smaller the prize.
The older the grudge, the keener the wrath.
The higher the cost, the lower the gain.

The weaker the foe, the shriller the cry.
The louder the lie, the further the truth.
The lighter the sword, the braver the knight.
The wilder the shot, the redder the stain.

Poet's note: These are not laws written in stone. They are sixteen mere assertions. Are they all true? I believe so, but I could be wrong. That's why I think it would be interesting to choose a line—one that strikes you as perhaps odd or altogether wrong—and do a little research to see if you can come up with an exception to the "rule."

Poems for Teaching in the Content Areas by J. Patrick Lewis   Scholastic Teaching Resources

Geography

Suggestions for Teaching With the Geography Poems

In the twenty-first century, instant communication has created a global society. That's why it's more important than ever for students to know their geography, including where places are on the globe and how diverse cultures can be. However, geography seems to be a weakness among American students. These poems will heighten students' interest in learning about the world; in natural disasters such as tsunamis, which can change the shape of the land and affect people across political borders; in natural formations such as coral reefs; and in remote yet inspiring places such as Angkor Wat. The section ends with haiku riddles for each of the fifty states in the U.S. We've included a map of the United States for students to use in conjunction with the haikus.

> *You may also want to check out these poems from the Science section:*
>
> "Said the Little Stone" (page 72)
>
> "The Lithosphere" (page 74)
>
> "Hurricane" (page 75)

Student Projects and Writing Ideas

Explore maps along with the values and lifestyles of other cultures by using these poems to dig deeper into and learn more about physical and cultural geography.

Preserving Our Earth

Read "Okefenokee Swamp Song" and focus on the issue of keeping large tracts of land safe in National Parks. Do research on the Internet to learn about the controversy surrounding using National Park land in Alaska to drill for oil. Or use the Internet to learn about problems and issues surrounding other National Parks and create a list of ways that you, your peers, and adults can keep this land safe for future generations.

Solve the Haiku Riddle

As an ongoing project, work with a partner to try to solve the riddles of "HaikUSA." As you solve each riddle, place the answer on a map of the United States.

Map a Coral Reef

After reading "How Coral Reefs Are Made From Tiny Animals (Polyps) Not Much Bigger Than a Pinhead," research coral reefs on the Internet. Use what you learn to design an illustrated and labeled map of a coral reef. When you present your map to the class, explain why it's important to preserve the coral reefs around the world and how these reefs impact the oceans and people.

Dig Into Culture

Choose one or two places mentioned in "Mapping the World" and find out more about each one. In addition to including an original illustration or one from the Internet, write up what you learned about these places or peoples. Share with your classmates in an oral presentation.

Writing Ideas

Research and/or use what you've learned in your class to transform facts into poems. Share these with classmates by reading them aloud or posting them on a bulletin board.

1. **Create a Shaped Poem.** Read "Tsunami" and notice how the poem's shape reflects the growing size of the tsunami wave. Write a shaped poem for another natural disaster that changes the physical geography of an area. Choose to write about a tornado, a hurricane, an earthquake, or a volcanic eruption.

2. **Put On a Geographical Mask.** Choose a geographical feature, such as a mountain, a glacier, the ocean, a desert, a swamp, a river, or a volcano, and become that thing. Brainstorm a list of ideas to use in a poem that expresses ideas from the point of view of the geographical feature. Include issues that affect you, such as global warming's effect on glaciers, the pollution of oceans and rivers, and so on. Then, illustrate the poem with photographs, original drawings, or images from the Internet.

3. **Geography Haiku.** A haiku is a poem with 17 syllables spread among three lines in this pattern: first line, 5 syllables; second line, 7 syllables; third line, 5 syllables. Write a haiku about the physical aspects of natural formations you've seen, such as a geyser, a waterfall, a plateau, a sound, a river, or a pond. You might consider writing about a photograph, original drawing, or image from the Internet.

Okefenokee Swamp Song

Southern Georgia/Northern Florida

The panthers run
And the alligators sun
Themselves in the Okefenokee,
Where the cypress smoke
And the frogs go croaking
Down in the Okefenokee.

It's a National Park
So thick and dark
The dogs step backward just to bark
Down in the Okefenokee.
From longleaf pine
Drips turpentine,
And folks sure love the monkeyshine
Down in the Okefenokee.

Old Spanish moss
Sweeps heaps across
A swamp the color of Worcestershire sauce
Down in the Okefenokee.
On gallberry honey
You make a little money—
Git, got gone by Saturday, sonny,
Down in the Okefenokee,
Down in the black-brown watery town
Known as the Okefenokee.

Tsunami

Ordinary sea waves are whipped by the winds.

Tidal waves occur when the Moon begins

its gravitational pull against the Earth.

But have you noticed how oddly the ocean behaves?

A tsunami is the most devastating of all waves!

100 miles long! An earthquake gives birth

to enormous explosions of gas and rock!

Which is why tsunamis come

as something of a

SHOCK!

Poems for Teaching in the Content Areas by J. Patrick Lewis   Scholastic Teaching Resources

El Niño

Heats up the ocean,
Turns on the fan
Folks can feel
In Pakistan.
Africa dries up,
Canada freezes,
Australia's allergic,
Europe sneezes.

He's the bully "boy"
All year,
Taking the heat
For the atmos-fear.

How Coral Reefs Are Made From Tiny Animals (Polyps) Not Much Bigger Than a Pinhead

A polyp
Will crawl up
And doll up
The reef.

Sea floor'll
Be coral
Of floral-
like leaf.

Postcard in
A garden
Boneyard in
The sea,

Whose view is
For you as
Deep blue as
Can be.

Poems for Teaching in the Content Areas by J. Patrick Lewis   Scholastic Teaching Resources

Dusk, a Back Porch, Canada

Shy Evening paints all heaven gray,
Erasing blue from Balmy Day,

Uncolors brute box elders, oaks,
And elms with even, gentle strokes,

Then finds the houses, whereupon
She dabs her brush . . . their lights come on

As if two dozen stars fell down
To twinkle life into the town.

But Evening's easel leaves undone
One mischief streak of Western Sun

That graces the masterpiece she drew—
"Still Life: An Evening's Point of View"—

Till he robs her of fading light,
That thief of art, Black-hearted Night.

First Photograph Ever Taken
By a Spacecraft of Planet Earth

From U.S. Lunar Orbiter 1
August 23, 1966

When you see this first photograph
Of Mother Earth, this Otherwhere,
And then only the upper half . . .
What creatures could be living there?

A land of giants? Bright green elves?
Anyone that we might know?
If we could only see ourselves
In that fantastic picture show.

From this lunar horizon, there
Appears a cold and distant dome.
We pause, completely unaware,
Until we realize . . .
it's home.

Poems for Teaching in the Content Areas by J. Patrick Lewis   Scholastic Teaching Resources

In the South Pacific

The
world
divides
itself   in
two—emer-
ald green &
cornflower blue.
A white gullwing
drifts on the wind.
Beneath the Pacific's
mirror sky, alone on the
ocean's   distant   crease,

it sails this picture, rarely shown,
a divided world . . .
at peace.

Lives of the Explorers

Balboa's dog Leoncico
was first to reach the mountaintop
and gaze upon the Pacific.

John Cabot promised to give away
islands, even to his barber.

Magellan walked with a limp.
Columbus had red hair.
Marco Polo got homesick
but only after twenty years.

Amerigo Vespucci thought
Noah's Ark too small to hold
all the species of Brazil.

Ponce de Leon drank the sparkling
water from a spring on Key Biscayne,
thinking it would make him younger.
He was wrong.

Poems for Teaching in the Content Areas by J. Patrick Lewis   Scholastic Teaching Resources

First Man to Reach the South Pole

Roald Amundsen
Norwegian Explorer
December 14, 1911

They set out from the Bay of Whales
One afternoon of hope,
Five men on sleds and fifty-two dogs
Down to the southern slope.

Because two months would pass before
They reached the polar dome,
Cutting and stacking blocks of ice,
They marked their way back home.

A mountain range, 10,000 feet,
Protected that brass ring,
As if to dare Amundsen. But why
Yield to anything?

They ate seal cutlets, powdered milk
And chocolate to survive
Ice country none had ever known—
And barely stayed alive.

But at the Pole they planted Norway's
Flag in knee-deep snow,
And named the plain on which it lies
King Haakon VII's Plateau.

Tour Guide

Hey, girl, let's go to Europe,
we'll see Al sass Lorraine,

and just for something crazy
to do, we'll go in Seine!

If you and I go Turin,
we'll find a place to Rome

and Italy—'ven be our
home away from home.

The Taj Mahal

Have you ever wondered where the sun sleeps?
My house.

Do you know how white marble flatters heaven?
My domes.

Where can you see green geometry?
My gardens.

Pilgrim, where can you experience rapture?
My minarets.

Have you ever looked upon the jewelry of God?
My malachite, lapis and carnelian.

What is this monument to love and death?
My Mogul dream.

Poems for Teaching in the Content Areas by J. Patrick Lewis   Scholastic Teaching Resources

Stonehenge

Salisbury Plain
Wiltshire, England

. . . and the artist said, *We should imitate*
the volcano, mountainously heaped.

And the ruffian warned, *It will take*
one hundred full moons to move a stone.

But our fathers are worth ten thousand-
weight, sang a voice from the scrub.

I must be able to reckon a darkness
shadowing the afternoon, mused Timekeeper,
for Moon and Sun to tell us of their travels.

Rope-weaver spoke, *We can expect no sympathy*
from the sea.

And the Beaker Folk, easy by the wood fires,
went on talking through the endless night.

Angkor Wat

In 1861 Henri Mouhot,
eager to find a rare white butterfly,
endured Cambodia's oppressive heat,
and stumbled on the Orient's Versailles.

The weeping ghost of Angkor Wat at last
defeated mist, liana vines and time—
four centuries had passed since anyone
observed this Khmer temple in its prime.

Cobras slithered on its colonnades,
panthers ruled its rooms, monkeys held court
on staircases. From towers acorn-shaped,
enormous fruit bats flapped as if for sport.

It's taken years—the task remains undone—
to clear a jungle that had swallowed such
magnificence. Monks, scholars, travelers still
marvel how time, that thief, could steal so much

Of Angkor Wat. And now what will you see?
A drama, starring Early Antiquity.

Poet's note: For sheer mystery, perhaps no other historical site can match Angkor Wat. Located in the heart of Cambodia's densest jungles, its huge pyramid structure is the highest achievement of Khmer temple architecture, dating back to as early as 200 C.E. Hidden from Western eyes for much of its existence, Angkor Wat resembles Hindu and Buddhist temples, owing to the influence of early Indian and Chinese settlers.

Poems for Teaching in the Content Areas by J. Patrick Lewis   Scholastic Teaching Resources

Fallingwater

Bear Run, Pennsylvania, 1936–1937
Architect: Frank Lloyd Wright

When I first saw
This mystic house,
The Blue Danube
By Johann Strauss

Is what I heard
From where I stood,
Resounding through
The silent wood,

Because this house
Is, after all,
The music of
A waterfall.

Separately, water
And abode—
Together they
Had ebbed and flowed

So perfectly
I knew I knew
What greatness was
Supposed to do.

Poet's note: In 1986, the *New York Times* architecture critic wrote: "This is a house that summed up the 20th century and then thrust it forward still further.... It is [architect Frank Lloyd Wright's] most sublime integration of man and nature." Designed and built in 1936–37 for a department store owner, Fallingwater actually rises over a waterfall and has been called "one of the complete masterpieces of twentieth century art."

Mapping the World

I took my nibs to *Africa*
Because a fire was in my brain,
And sharpened them acacia-fine
To paint the Serengeti Plain,
Victoria Falls, a River Nile
Meandering past ancient folk.
This continent foreshadows all
The colors of a master's stroke.

When I had laid out *Europe* on
A canvas, it would teach me much
About such glories of a past
I painted Russian, Greek and Dutch.
In pencil on my drawing board,
I traced *Australia*'s seamless land—
Dreamtime of Aborigines,
A walkabout through scrub and sand.

Let my skilled pen alone express
The thrill when *Asia* asked me in
To map astonishment for here
Great Walls and history begin.
From fields of rice, my leap of faith
To fields of ice, you hear me shout
Antarctica!—pale continent.
My white ink practically ran out.

Which leaves me now to picture this:
I paint great nations lying South,
Canada and the fifty states.
Out of the wide, wide river's mouth—
Americas, Americas!—
Although the ink is not dry yet.
Geography is like our own
Room with a view we can't forget.

Poet's note: Thanks to Lee Bennett Hopkins, in whose anthology *Got Geography* (Greenwillow, 2006) this poem first appeared.

52

Poems for Teaching in the Content Areas by J. Patrick Lewis   Scholastic Teaching Resources

The Meaning(s) of Geography

Land of honest men—Burkina Faso

People of the ten arrows—Hungary

Land of a thousand hills—Rwanda

Land of a million elephants—Laos

Island of the moon—Comoros

Land of forty tribes—Kyrgyzstan

Land of the pure—Pakistan

Land of castles—Catalonia

Abundance of butterflies—Panama

Land of the hummingbird—Trinidad

Land of the eagle—Albania

Land of the lions—Sri Lanka

Land of silver—Argentina

There was gold—Aruba

Land of the thunder dragon—Bhutan

Land of flaming water—Malawi

Land of the blacks—the Sudan

Big house of stone—Zimbabwe

Land of the angles—England

Land of free men—France

Land of the rising sun—Japan

Land of self-masters—Uzbekistan

End of the earth—Madagascar

Land of nothing—Namibia

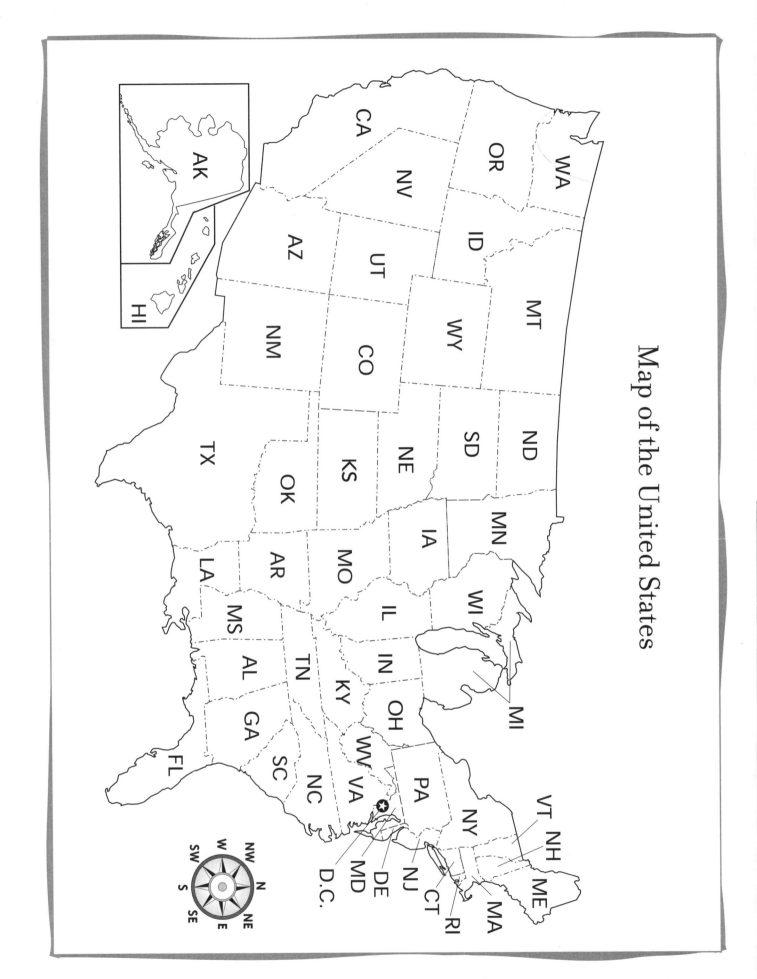

Map of the United States

Poems for Teaching in the Content Areas by J. Patrick Lewis   Scholastic Teaching Resources

HaikUSA (1)

1.

My capital is
a car, a penny and a
U.S. President

2.

In 1903
I was the first state to take
flight. Isn't that Wright?

3.

An anagram for
nominates contains the most
Scandinavians

4.

Girl, tin man, scarecrow,
lion near my capital—
I'm *a pet, ok?*

5.

O had I a hoe
I'd go hoe potato rows—
Your good pal(indrome)

6.

We've got cactus, we've
got heat, and we've got a great
big hole in the ground

7.

People may take me
"for granite" but I was first
to break from England

8.

My huskies and *I
did it, a r*ousing sled ride
through the biggest state

9.

I have more cows than
any state (and you'll find *cows*
mixed up in my name)

10.

Home to Little League,
cheesesteak sandwich, chocolate
and shady groundhogs

HaikUSA (2)

11.

I am snow-covered
bighorn sheep grazing on the
rocky road to fame

12.

Somewhere in these hills
and woods *Eva is writing—*
no, wait, revising!

13.

Inside me you are
within eighty-five miles of
one of the Great Lakes

14.

One of my glitzy
towns has more hotel rooms than
any place on earth

15.

Home of Superman—
and I was once very Abe-
ly represented

16.

Suppose the U.S.
were an Empire . . . you could see
me scraping the sky

17.

The first slave state to
free its slaves—home to iced tea
and the ice cream cone!

18.

State with the fewest
people, but say Hi to Shy
Anne and Lara Mie

19.

My capital shares
the same name, Chris, as that oh
so great explorer

20.

Motto: *EUREKA!*
(I have found it!)—the lowest
point and the highest

Answers: 11. Colorado; 12. West Virginia; 13. Michigan; 14. Nevada; 15. Illinois; 16. New York; 17. Missouri; 18. Wyoming; 19. Ohio (Columbus); 20. California

Poems for Teaching in the Content Areas by J. Patrick Lewis   Scholastic Teaching Resources

HaikUSA (3)

21.

I ramble to my
biggest city . . . once I got
there I *ran madly*

22.

From the nine letters
in my name, take away "ten"—
and you're left with six

23.

My biggest claim to
fame rocks the world—no legs, four
dynamite faces

24.

If you have been to
visit me, my capital
proved nice, didn't it?

25.

Think of Daniel Boone,
think of gold—and a place where
great horses are foaled

26.

Sooner or later
everyone should visit my
Cowboy Hall of Fame

27.

There's lots of music
in my capital, three words
with four letters each

28.

01001—
first U.S. Postal zip code
is at Agawam

29.

Over a thousand
people per square mile are packed
into this "new" state

30.

My motto is "The
Crossroads of America"—
"Land of Indians"

HaikUSA (4)

31.

Aw, shucks, *I send some*
corny capital greetings
from barn-farm central

32.

You should be able
to "connect" me with Yankee
Doodle, my state song

33.

Largest producer
of maple syrup, I am
French for "Green Mountains"

34.

Two great presidents
built their homes here—Mt. Vernon
and Monticello

35.

Although I'm under
Ten, I stand next to a Miss—
Also over Flo

36.

Only state with a
Small stone right in the middle
For its capital

37.

My legislature
Has debateD over anD
Over anD over

38.

Whenever we go
to this state's largest city
I'm hungry—Let's eat!

39.

Vacation with me!
The only state with two i's
Close to each other

40.

I'm home to gators,
Waders, great grandpaters and
Great-great grandmaters

Answers: 31. Iowa; 32. Connecticut; 33. Vermont; 34. Virginia; 35. Alabama; 36. Arkansas (Little Rock); 37. Delaware (Dover); 38. Washington (Seattle); 39. Hawaii; 40. Florida

Poems for Teaching in the Content Areas by J. Patrick Lewis   Scholastic Teaching Resources

HaikUSA (5)

41.

You can *go far*, kid!
And if you get that *far, go*
Into Canada

42.

Some tourists say the
Best anagram for me is,
Oh coastal ruin!

43.

You will discover
A peachy *org* right in the
Middle of my name

44.

Guess where? *Once we mix*
Aztecs, Spaniards, and paintings
By Georgia O'Keeffe

45.

Where *Tom, Anna* meet
With *Nat, Mona*—together
Under the big sky

46.

Son, we learn a lot
About spicy Cajun food
In this jazzy place

47.

I mean; a mine; I
Name; i.e., man—take your pick,
I am near the north

48.

Males OR females go
Round the Bend to reach the coast
Love it here, Eugene!

49.

I am not for N,
But I'm for S's, for I's
And P's, too. Get it?

50.

The first word spoken
From the Moon is a city
In my giant state

Science

Suggestions for Teaching With the Science Poems

A friend who is a physicist repeatedly tells me that science is poetry. Look at a snowflake, a crystal, fog, a tree through the seasons, photographs of planets and super novas—her examples are endless. This marriage between science and poetry will make sharing these science poems with your students a memorable experience for them. My hope is that, like Pat, your students will be inspired to craft poems about topics that speak to them as well as learn more about the subjects of these poems.

> *You may also want to check out these poems from the Geography section:*
>
> "Tsunami" (page 40)
>
> "El Niño" (page 41)
>
> "How Coral Reefs Are Made From Tiny Animals (Polyps) Not Much Bigger Than a Pinhead" (page 42)

Student Projects and Writing Ideas

You can explore these suggestions on the Internet, by reading library books, and by interviewing your science teacher or other science experts. Share your research with classmates.

All the Spheres

After reading "The Lithosphere," research the "spheres" that make up the atmosphere on earth and on the sun. Draw and label a diagram of these. Then research the greenhouse effect and the changes scientists see in the atmosphere. Explain the issues surrounding the greenhouse effect and how these impact you and the lives of all people.

For or Against Genetic Engineering

Use "Chromosome Poem" as a springboard for exploring the controversies around the genetic engineering of fruits and vegetables. Find information on the Internet, interview adults and peers, and use the data you've collected to take a position for or against the genetic engineering of fruits and vegetables. Transform your data into an opinion paragraph or a letter to the editor of your local newspaper.

Guide to Space Travel

Prepare a virtual tour of our solar system by drawing each planet. Then take your classmates for a ride through space explaining the topography of each planet and how each was discovered.

Celebrate Cells

Read "Fifty Million Million Cells" and investigate single-celled organisms or specialized cells in humans and animals, such as muscle, heart, blood, nerve, and skin cells. Illustrate 2–3 cell types or single-celled organisms and write about them. Include as many fascinating facts as you can find.

Writing Ideas

Read your poems to your classmates and/or arrange them on a bulletin board.

1. **It Can't Talk Back.** Write a poem about something in science that can't talk back, such as a cell, the moon, a bat, a black hole, a comet, or a giant squid. For models, read "Said the Little Stone" and "The Loneliest Creature." These are called apostrophe poems. Brainstorm a list of ideas from the point of view of the scientific thing you choose, then write your poem.

2. **Find the Heart of It.** Look closely at a snowflake, a crystal, a chemical change, a rock, a motor, or a lunar eclipse and write a poem that shows you have pinpointed the beauty and poetry in science. These poems will provide excellent models for you to study: "Fifty Million Million Cells" and "The Xerces Blue."

3. **Shape It!** Read "Why Leaves Change Color in the Fall." Notice that the poem is written in the shape of a tree. Think of something science-related that you'd like to write a poem about, such as a shark, a spacecraft, a black hole, a comet, an ameba or paramecium, and so on, and write a poem in the shape of what you choose.

What Is Science?

Science is a mathematician walking down the hall
of an equation

Science is an astronaut repairing Hubble

Science is the next Einstein, wild eyes, wilder hair,
hooked on String Theory

Science is an oceanographer avoiding the hammerheads

Science is a spelunker, friend of cave bats

Science is a chemist lost in the scent of a new perfume

Science is a hurricane tracker driving like the wind

Science is a sleeper, electrodes to dreamscapes

Science is an environmentalist, instruments to icecaps

Science is a navigator charting the distance to landfall

Science is a teacher explaining why the sky is blue

Science is a student, his third place prize on chordates
at the Science Fair

Science is an astronomer in a fever of anticipation . . .
an unnamed star

Poems for Teaching in the Content Areas by J. Patrick Lewis   Scholastic Teaching Resources

The Great Divide

Now we come to the Great Divide
(*Mitosis*) when a "parent cell"
Breaks into two more cells (or "daughters").
Think of them as parallel.

Some daughter cells are like their parent,
Number of chromosomes the same.
But some of them split further—that's
Meiosis (scientific name)—

With half the parent's chromosomes.
And how they love to wiggle and squirm,
Those microscopic daughters who
Become the *gametes* (eggs or sperm).

Chromosome Poem

Each chromosome is home
To many genes
(The body's biological machines)
That tell you if your eyes
Are brown or blue,
Determine sizes
Of your hat, your shoe,

And tell you if your hair
Will wave or frizz.
The chromosomes sort out
The Hers from His
By making you
A Mr. or a Ms.

Poems for Teaching in the Content Areas by J. Patrick Lewis   Scholastic Teaching Resources

Fifty Million Million Cells

Fifty million million cells
Are bundled in you and me.
But most of nature's creatures
Can climb the family tree
With just one cell, and so,
Impossible to see,
Adapt so well we are
Content to let them be.

They set off no alarms,
They ring no sudden bells.
They dwell in dust, in ponds,
Or under beds. Some cells
Contain a nucleus,
A range of organelles,
While others—bacteria—
Can cast invisible spells.

How numberless are these?
Like sand under the seas.

Why Leaves Change Color in the Fall

I was just about
to explain to my class that leaves are
nature's food factories taking water from the
ground and carbon dioxide from the air and using
sunlight to turn water and carbon dioxide into glucose
a kind of sugar that gives a tree its energy through
a process called photosynthesis which is helped along by
a chemical known as chlorophyll that makes trees and
plants green though during the winter photosynthesis
does not work as efficiently due to less water and shorter
hours of daylight so trees begin to shut down their food
factories and green chlorophyll-filled leaves take a holiday
by turning themselves yellow and orange and that maple
tree for instance where the glucose is trapped in the
leaves now that photosynthesis has stopped
begins to turn into a glorious scarlet …
but then I thought why take the
time to explain it when
I could
just sit
here and
watch the
wonders
of leaves
changing
colors be-
fore they
all fall to
t   h   e   g   r   o   u   n   d

Poems for Teaching in the Content Areas by J. Patrick Lewis   Scholastic Teaching Resources

The Greenhouse Effect

From the Sun's
Blazing rays,
Heat arrives
Here it stays.

Atmosphere
Traps the heat,
Bakes the fields,
Warms the street.

With no Green-
House effect,
Winter would
Go unchecked,

But our gray
Polluted skies
Could cause temp-
Eratures to rise.

Butterfly to Butterfly

She finds a spot. Her stay is brief
She lays her egg beneath a leaf.

Inside the egg, day after day,
A caterpillar has a way

Of knowing how to stretch and grow.
Once on her own, she likes to show

The kind of trick that nature brings,
And like her Mother, spread her WINGS!

Poems for Teaching in the Content Areas by J. Patrick Lewis   Scholastic Teaching Resources

The Xerces Blue

Glaucopsyche xerces
Not seen since 1943
San Francisco

She butters up a piece of western sky,
Your *ooh*-and-*ahh*some cousin butterfly,
But you, could you be hiding in the shade
Flapping to a spotted sister on a blade
Of grass? Watching ants sipping at a pond?
High-flown forever to the Blue Beyond?

Did drivers ever witness at rush hour
The last of you unfasten from a flower?
The world explodes in colors, but a few
Still miss your royal Xerces shade of blue.

Note: The French entomologist Boisduval named the butterfly for the Persian king Xerxes (486–465 B.C.), but used the French spelling, Xerces.

The Loneliest Creature

"Lonesome George"
The only surviving Pinta tortoise
currently living on the island of Santa Cruz

I cannot talk but to the wind,
I cannot play the old shell game,
I cannot see far out to sea.
I heard a voice, but no one came.

What fate awaits a ragged king
Beyond the dunes—a rugged climb?
The seasons change too late, too soon;
I have too much, too little time.

Poems for Teaching in the Content Areas by J. Patrick Lewis   Scholastic Teaching Resources

Said Father Owl to Junior Owl

Leap into the wind and beat your wings!
As wings press down (those feathery things),

They push against the air, of course,
Creating—*whoosh*—an upward force

That's stronger than your body weight
(For which air has to compensate).

Now as wings flap, the air will pass
Between your feathers, soft as grass.

And this is what cuts down resistance,
Which lets you go the extra distance.

Okay now, Junior, mark my words:
This explanation's for the birds.

Said the Little Stone

I would like to thank you, Volcano,
for magma, mother of the island,
for fire that settled me under the sun,
and for the company of these three
delicate flowers, blowing, bowing
in their poetic photosynthetic joy.

I would like some day to fit
in the hand of Early Man, to be
tool, axe, charm, to skim a lake
of glass like a fisher bird, or,
if wind and water are willing,
to become a work of polished art.

I, little stone, would like to outlive
by millennia the Old Stone Age.

Poems for Teaching in the Content Areas by J. Patrick Lewis   Scholastic Teaching Resources

Only a Matter of Degrees

Our geography guru
Mrs. Cambruzzi's
doozy for the day:
"Say Earth is 24,902
miles in circumference
and there are 360
degrees in a circle.
The distance between
two lines of latitude
0 degrees to 1 degree
North—is how many
miles?"

Silence.

Nobody knows . . . until
this brainiac's
hand flies up
when a light goes on.

"It's 4 miles longer
than 2½ times the
length of a marathon."

Answer: 69.2 miles (24,902 divided by 360 = 69.2 miles)
A marathon race is approximately 26 miles. (2½ x 26) = 65 + 4 = 69 miles

The Lithosphere

The *lithosphere*, our solid Earth,
Can rotate gradually or shift
On plates (tectonic), if you catch
My continental drift.

Although it may be obvious now
That continents can float,
It seems absurd to think that every
Continent's a boat.

But plate tectonics isn't such
A radical idea
If you know what the Earth looked like
When it was called *Pangaea*.

Poems for Teaching in the Content Areas by J. Patrick Lewis   Scholastic Teaching Resources

Hurricane

When Wind puts into port from distant seas,
She may toss fishing boats about the bay
Or tie up at the docks without a stir
Or thunderstorm herself a right-of-way.

When Wind decides to corrugate the blue,
Agitating in white along the coast,
She ruins everybody's holiday.
Still, she may bellow forth a final boast

By galloping into a hurricane,
A terrifying Category Five:
One-hundred-sixty-mile-an-hour Winds
Beat down the town clinging to stay alive.

And after Mother Nature's mad machine
Begins to lose her breath once over land,
She leaves federal disaster at a scene
Survivors are too numb to understand.

The Aged Sun

Whether our star, the sun, grows old
By turning into liquid gold

And dripping down invisible space
To some celestial fireplace,

Expands, like science says it must,
And turns its planets into dust,

Or simply ups and disappears
Like some ascending-ending spheres,

I do not think it matters much.
Great things destroy, depart, lose touch

When slow time reckons they are done—
And so it will be with the sun,
And so it will be with the sun.

Poems for Teaching in the Content Areas by J. Patrick Lewis   Scholastic Teaching Resources

Driving to the Moon

If you drive to the Moon in your average car,
And you wonder how long the trip is and how far—
Here's the answer: At seventy miles per hour
In the family sedan with its average horsepower,
No skyway patrolmen out cruising for speeders,
No reason to feed flying parking meters.
Make sure you pack plenty of outer space food,
Star-carsickness pills for the high altitude.
Now to get to the Moon on the lunar highways
Will take you . . .

134 days!

The Big Bang

Well, we thank you, Edwin Hubble,
That you took the time and trouble
To investigate just how the world began—

Like a universal splatter,
An exploding pu-pu platter,
Or a zillion popcorn kernels in a pan.

How and why and when and whether
All the matter came together
Is a riddle not completely understood,

But there is a growing chorus—
Fifteen billion years before us,
Something definitely wrecked the neighborhood!

Poems for Teaching in the Content Areas by J. Patrick Lewis   Scholastic Teaching Resources

A Black Hole

A star that's just
Too fat to hang
Far out in space
May pop—and bang!

Its insides get
So blazing hot
One day it's there
The next it's not!

And no one knows
Exactly why
But in the ceiling
Of the sky,

The space that swallows
Starry light
Is big as day
And dark as night.

Five Simple Things You Can Do With the Five Simple Machines

Lift your cousin Trevor,
whatever,
with a **LEVER**.

What'll get you there faster?
Railroad tracks'll
by **WHEEL** and **AXLE**.

Become a skateboard champ.
Find a training camp
with a **RAMP**.

Jack up the back of a Mack truck
with the curlicue
of a **SCREW**.

Haul the fifth grade bully
into a gully
with a **PULLEY**.

Poems for Teaching in the Content Areas by J. Patrick Lewis   Scholastic Teaching Resources

Universagrams

Moon's light = Night looms = Gloom's hint

Astronaut = NASA tutor

Lunar eclipse = Peculiar lens

Shooting star = Soars tonight!

Apollo landing site = Spot in Galileo Land

The Aurora Borealis = Has too rare blue air

Halley's Comet = Yes, call me hot!

Neil Armstrong = Normal gent, sir

Black hole = Hello back!

Crab Nebula = Can be a blur

Cloud formation= Um, a cold tin roof?

Asteroid = It soared!

Streaks of lightning = A night fork glistens

Sea of Tranquility = Afar, it's only quiet

Stratosphere = Earth's poster

Ozone layer = Nearly ooze

Sally K. Ride = I'll dare sky

Solar eclipse = All too precise

Communications satellite = COMSAT: Metallic noise unit

Hurricane Andrew = Churned air…*we ran!*

The Royal Observatory = Oh boy, starry elevator!

SPIRIT Rover = Trip over, sir

Moon's gravity = A moving story

The meteor shower = The more the worse

The Space Station = No escape, that's it

The flight of Icarus = Graceful if hottish

Tornado watch = Hard to act now

Booster rocket = Erect robots, ok?

The equator = Heat torque

Over the rainbow = Borrow it, heaven

The Space Shuttle = Set up steel hatch

Stratus clouds = Stardust locus

Lunar module = A modern lulu

Outer space = A true scope = Escape tour

Math

Suggestions for Teaching With the Math Poems

When I shared these poems with several math teachers I know, they were enthusiastic about bringing them into their classroom and reading them to students. Here are the reasons these teachers wanted to offer these poems to their students:

- It's great for students to see problems as part of poetry—literature.

- These will surprise and intrigue students, because this will probably be their first encounter with math as poetry.

- I want students to see that math can inspire a writer to create poems about topics they study.

Including poetry in your math classroom can inspire students to write original math problem poems and show them that problem solving, a creative process, can be part of a literary genre. Encourage students to write their own math-problem poems or poems that express their feelings toward algebra, geometry, rational numbers, problem solving, and so on.

> *You may also want to check out these poems from the Science section:*
>
> "Only a Matter of Degrees" (page 73)
>
> "Driving to the Moon" (page 77)

Poems for Teaching in the Content Areas by J. Patrick Lewis   Scholastic Teaching Resources

Student Projects and Writing Ideas

You can add a dash of excitement and creativity to your math studies by completing the activities that follow or others that you suggest. Share what you've learned with classmates.

Solve the Math Poems

Work with a partner to read and solve two to four of the poems. Explain your solutions, using words, under the poem, then post on a bulletin board.

Create an Anthology of Math Poems

Choose five to six math problem poems, then illustrate and solve each one on a separate piece of paper. Create a title and dedication page and a page for a table of contents. Design a cover that celebrates math and poetry and staple your anthology, creating a book to share with classmates and other classes.

Design an Illustrated Math Terminology Dictionary

Make a math dictionary by selecting terms such as *integers, random numbers, exponents, probability, decimals,* and so on. Decide, with the help of your teacher, how many terms to write, explain, and illustrate.

Create a Web Site for Math Enthusiasts

Design a math Web site that contains your favorite J. P. Lewis poems, comments about the poems by you and your peers, and original math poems you and classmates have written.

Writing Ideas

Your challenge is to embed a math problem into a poem by combining numbers, concepts, and words. Read and share your poem with classmates and ask them to solve the problem.

1. **Alphabet Math Poem.** Read "The Math Abecedarian." Now write your own math ABC poem.

2. **Shape That Poem.** Read "What's My Angle?" and notice that the poem is in the shape of an angle. Create a poem in the shape of one of these: a trapezoid, a square, a rectangle, a circle, or a right or isosceles triangle. First brainstorm a list of ideas you can use, then share these with a partner to gather a few more. Now draft a poem that describes the geometric shape you've chosen.

3. **Rap Your Way Into Math.** Write a math rap about a specific topic and perform it. First brainstorm a list of ideas to include in your rap, then choose those that you want to include.

As I Walked Out One Evening

As I walked out one evening,
Down Mathematical Street,
A Gang—the Random Numbers—
Discrete but not discreet,

Ran into the Fraction Faction,
Scourge of Triangle Square.
They drew their mighty pencils—
Such algebrave warfare!—

Until the Fraction Faction,
Reduced to the lowest terms
And dragging its remainders,
Squared off with the Angleworms.

A gaggle of Integers gathered—
See Random Numbers mount!—
As some marched to infinity
And some went down for the count.

Coordinates in Ordered Pairs
Point to the crowd and laugh.
They stand in a line with a ± sign
For a go at a grid of a graph.

Opponents meet exponents
To the power of 2 or 3
Like the Gang of Random Numbers
In all probability.

Poems for Teaching in the Content Areas by J. Patrick Lewis   Scholastic Teaching Resources

A Field Guide to the Numbers

The Zero: lives alone, but often socializes with the other Integers.

The One-half: survives best at 2 below; on the whole, it comes up short.

The One: likes the single life; when it multiplies or divides, nothing happens.

The Dozen: lays its eggs in cartons; divides its time more or less equally throughout the year.

The Hundred: in its adult stage, is often confused with The Thousand.

The Googol: a rare bird; The Hundred perches on top of The Ten.

The Googolplex: the enormous nesting ground of The Zeroes.

Infinity: bears a strong resemblance to The Eight in its dormant state.

Inequalities

If > means greater than

and < means less than,

it stands to reason, man,

that if ≤ means less than or equal to

then this must be the sequel to

≥ which is _____.

In the Soccer Locker Room

In the room
full of 19
soccer players,
6 are 5'10",
7 are 5'6",
5 are 5'8",
but wait . . .
that leaves you
at 5'2",
the only one
on the scene
who can calculate
the mode,
the median
and the mean.

Poems for Teaching in the Content Areas by J. Patrick Lewis   Scholastic Teaching Resources

The Math Abecedarian

As Mr. Peter "Pi"
Bernoulli was
Correcting the test of
Danisha Hastings
Easily the brightest
Fifth grader at Horace
Greeley Middle School,
He came upon this problem:
"Ira opened
J.
K. Rowling's
Latest *Harry Potter* to Draco
Malfoy making fun of
Neville Longbottom. If the sum
Of the facing pages was 249, what
Pages did Ira open to?
(Question is worth 10 points)." Mr. Bernoulli
Read Danisha's answer: "The
Solution is to divide by
Two (which gives 124.5) and round
Up and down by a half. Pages 124 and 125."
Virtually every Danisha answer was perfect.
Wow! he thought. So he
Xeroxed her test to show the class, "What
You, you, and you can do when you're in the
Zone."

The Big Tipper

After an expensive lunch, Ben saw
The bill, which came to $45.02.
His buddy Rob said it should be a law
To leave a tip, which Ben said he would do.

The waitress was especially nice, the food
Was pretty good, so Ben thought, *What the heck*,
And being in a charitable mood,
He slyly slipped a ten under the check.

"Okay, big spender," Rob said, "what was that?"
"A ten," Ben said. "No, that's not what I meant.
Not the dollar amount, but what percent?"
"I wouldn't know," Ben said, "right off the bat."

How generous was Ben? (I'll bet the bus-
y waitress knows the answer to the quiz!)

Answer: The dollar amount of the tip ($10.00) divided by the dollar amount of the bill ($45.02) = 22.2% tip

Poems for Teaching in the Content Areas by J. Patrick Lewis   Scholastic Teaching Resources

The High Price of a New York New Year

I wanted to ring in New Year's Eve
on Times Square, but it was 10:20 p.m.
and I was 150 miles away flying down
the Interstate in my new Batmobile
look-alike with Lana (my ace navigator).
"Lana," I said, "how fast do I have
to drive for us to see the big ball fall
in Manhattan at midnight?" Lana
pulled out her abacus, and did a few
quick calculations, so I stepped on it!

That's when I heard the siren.

"Listen, Bat dude," the cop grinned.
"Just how fast do you and Batgirl
think you were going back there?"

Lana, who never tells a lie, told
the state patrolman just how fast.

"Happy New Year," he said,
and handed me a ticket for $250—
or $10 for ever mile over
the 65 mph speed limit.

So tell me. How fast was I going?

Answer: Since speed = distance over time, x =150 miles divided by 1.67 hours = 90 mph. Or $250 divided by $10 per mile = 25 miles over the speed limit (65) = 90 mph.

If I Were X

If I were **X** and you were **Y**,
I'd stand by you and . . . multiply.
And once the two of us were paired,
Why, they would call us $(XY)^2$.

If **Y** (that's you) were 1+2,
And $(XY)^2$ (that's me times you)
Were 36, what would be shown
As **X** (that's me), the great unknown?

A Monorhyme for Algebra

"No calculators, please," said Mr. Nye.
"For lack of exercise, your brains will die!
The pencil is the friend of X and Y.
Solve these tricky equations. Multiply,
Divide and take the square root. Now show why
Misplaced parentheses can falsify
The answer. *No! Not there, Melissa (sigh).*
Reduce that long solution. Simplify.
Tomorrow, decimals. There's the bell. Good-bye."

Poems for Teaching in the Content Areas by J. Patrick Lewis   Scholastic Teaching Resources

Idle Thought

what I like about
M. L. King Middle
School is that
math is so much
less painful than
brain surgery or
the root canal I
thought it would
be and it's all
because of
Mrs. DiPietro
who starts out
class by saying
that an anagram
for "Equations"
is "A Question"
so you should
never be afraid
to ask one or two
or X number of
questions where
X is equal to
$(16Y-20)$ when
Y is 2 and by the
time she gets
finished writing
that on the board
I've already figured
out that the answer
is just a minute
I'm thinking
12 I say out loud
to Mrs. D. nodding
over my shoulder

What's My Angle?

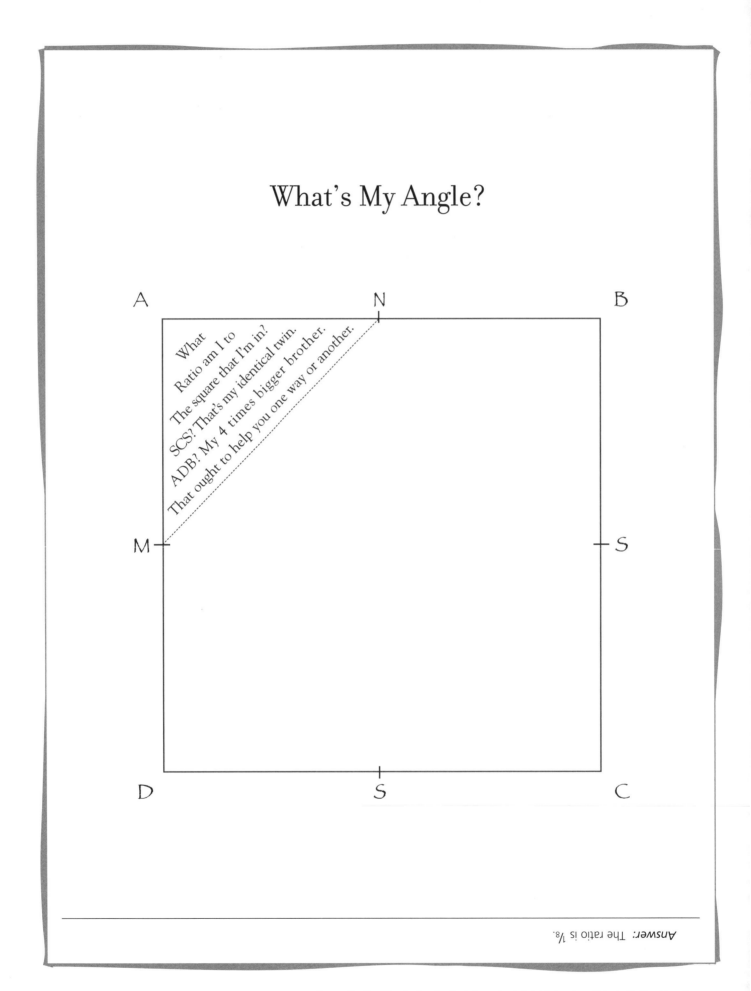

A · · · · · N · · · · · B

What
Ratio am I to
The square that I'm in?
SCS? That's my identical twin.
ADB? My 4 times bigger brother.
That ought to help you one way or another.

M

S

D · · · · · S · · · · · C

Poems for Teaching in the Content Areas by J. Patrick Lewis   Scholastic Teaching Resources

Seize the C's

$$40 = C + 2C - 101$$

Can you see what the C ought to be?
It's a mystery that bamboozles me.

Should I add, multiply or divide?
If so, where and how much and which side?

Well, maybe I'll wait and ask Kevin,
Mathematical whiz, Grade 7.

Answer: Add C + 2C = 3C; add 101 to both sides; that will give you 141 = 3C; divide 3 into both sides; therefore, C = 47.

The Rose Garden

I built a garden, 6' x 9',
To plant a bed of roses
And put a fence around the bed.
Now what do you suppose is
The length of wire I had to buy
To fit around the area,
Which now includes delphiniums,
Petunias and wisteria?

I stretched a piece of plastic over it
But very neatly.
How large (in square feet) was the piece
To cover it completely?

Answer: 6' + 6' + 9' + 9' = 30' = perimeter; 6' x 9' = 54 square feet.

Leftover Pizza

after William Carlos Williams (1883–1963)

The 10" square pizza
sliced in 2" squares
was so hot and tasty

I couldn't resist
eating 18 $\frac{1}{2}$ pieces.

Forgive me, Carlos.
You were hungry too.
I put the rest
in the refrigerator

Beside the white chickens,
but I forgot how much
pizza was left.

Poems for Teaching in the Content Areas by J. Patrick Lewis   Scholastic Teaching Resources

Side by Side by Side

A Hexagon went rolling down the street
And bumped into a Heptagon, who cried,
"Good morning, Hex? So nice that we should meet.
How would you like to see my better side?"
A Pentagon and Decagon stopped there
(It was a polygonish sort of night),
And everyone heard Pentagon declare,
"Our angles, boys—acute, obtuse or right?
How many sides and angles can you find
In four of us combined? To shed some light
Requires a skinny linear sort of mind.
Let's ask the Triangle. She's pretty bright."
The moral: Math is how, what, when and why
By giving it the ol' geome-TRY.

A Song to Miss Dean

after John Betjeman (1906–1984)

Miss Jo Alice Dean, Miss Jo Alice Dean,
Reigning explaining mathematical queen,
Raising an integer—*wow!*—to a power
(Exponent) and all in the course of an hour,

Finding percentages, solving for X,
Then doing it over so everything checks.
There, taking a bite of an apple between
Two rational numbers is Jo Alice Dean.

She draws on emotion to draw on a graph.
Her absolute values? Too funny by half.
Then ziggy and zaggy geometry talk
Appears as a miracle written in chalk.

Miss Jo Alice Dean, Miss Jo Alice Dean,
How happy I am! Now I see what you mean!
The test is tomorrow, I think I'm prepared
For anything, even $(10x + 2)^2$.

She picks up her papers and heads for the door,
"Let none of you *ever* say math is a bore!"
She touches her brain, that mathematics machine,
The winking, still thinking Miss Jo Alice Dean.

Poems for Teaching in the Content Areas by J. Patrick Lewis   Scholastic Teaching Resources